Florals & Mandalas

ADULT COLORING BOOK FOR RELAXATION

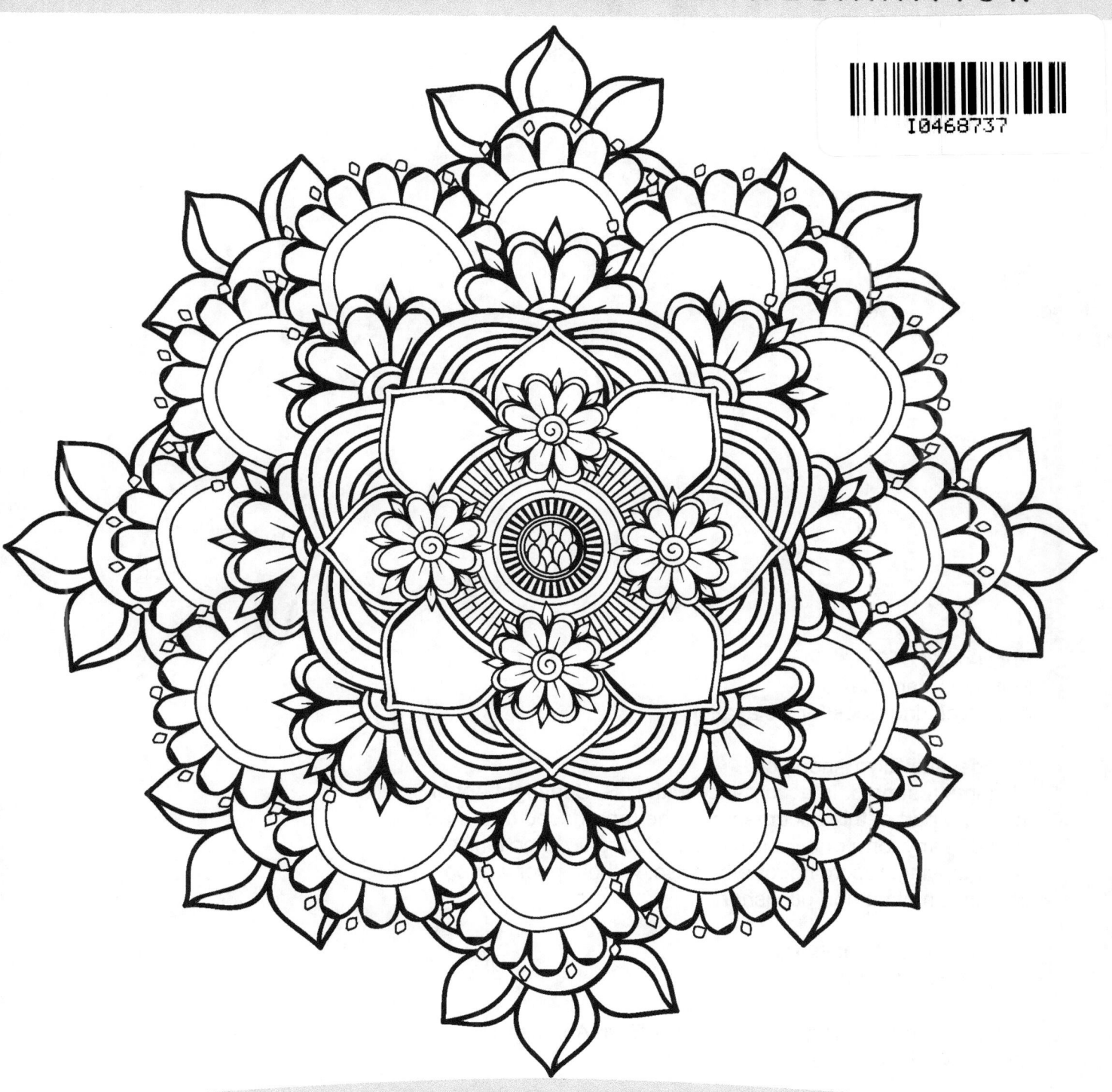

by Angelique Ellyn Anderson

Published 2016
Florals & Mandalas
Adult Coloring Book for Relaxation

ISBN-13:978-1530259410
ISBN-10:153025941X

Designed and illustrated by Angelique Ellyn Anderson
http://www.liquestudio.com

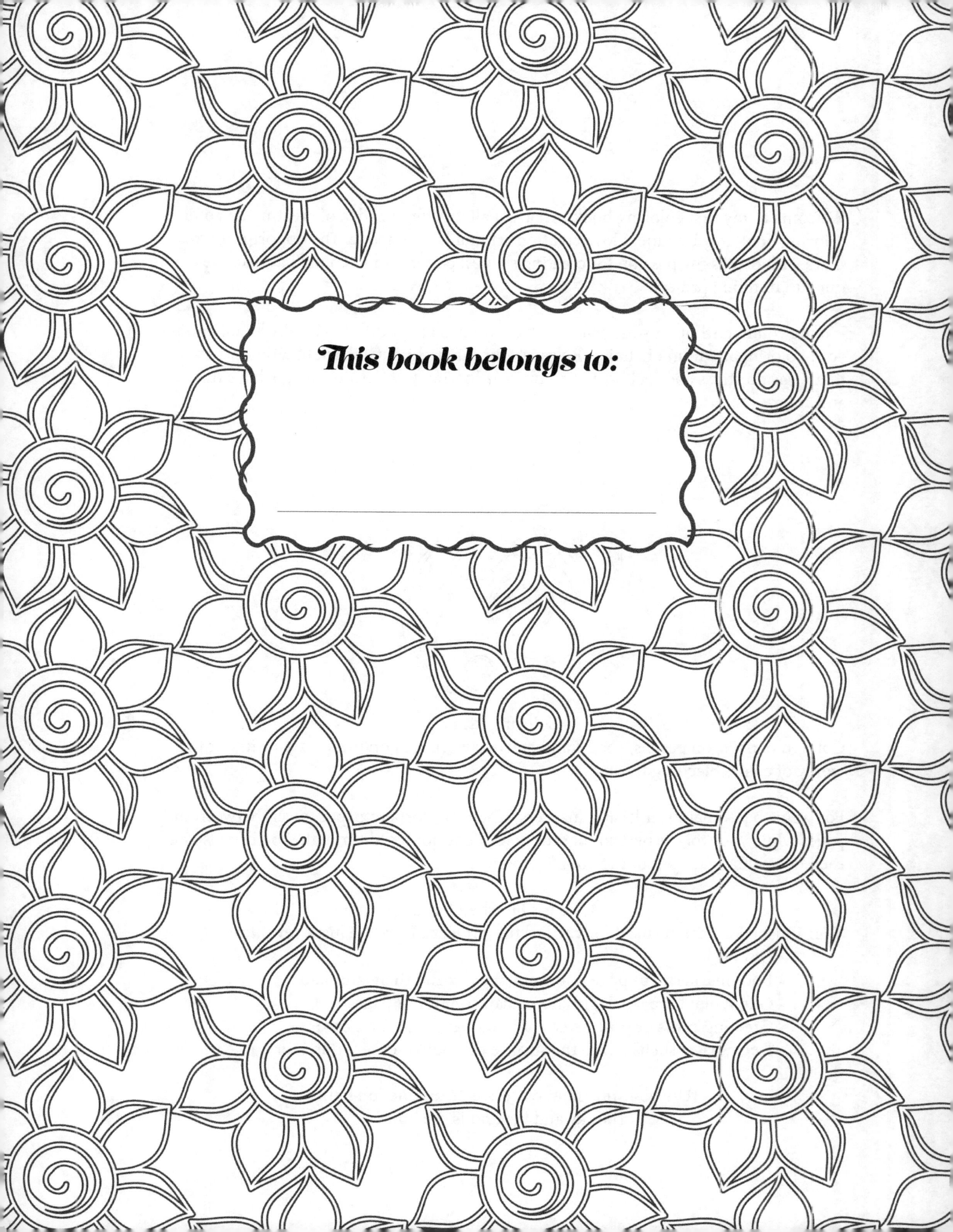

This book belongs to:

_____

Welcome to my first coloring book. An artist all my life, the idea of creating an adult coloring book inspired me; I love creating art that is interactive. The opportunity to share with others my passion for creating shapes, patterns, and colors has become a fun and fulfilling project.

I invite you to curl up in your favorite chair or relax at your desk with this book and your coloring medium of choice. Release your inner child. Go back to a time when there was no stress about choosing colors or adhering to rules. Just let go, have fun and color.

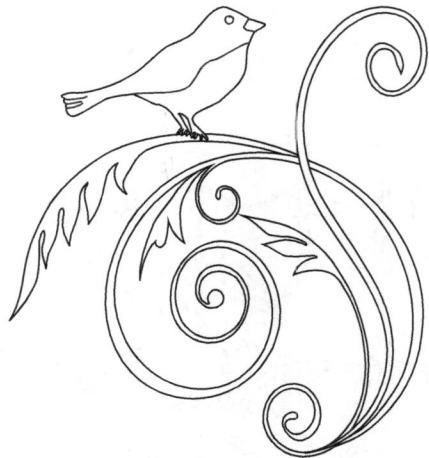

Coloring Ideas

Colored pencils, oil pastels, chalks and crayons work well on these pages without the worry of colors bleeding through.

For water-based paints, inks and markers, placing absorbent paper towels between the pages while you work is best so that the color does not bleed through. You can also cut each individual page out of the book to color.

Uses for Finished Pages

Your finished art can be used for various fun projects. Here are just a few ideas.

- Gift tags
- Bookmarkers: cut page into 4 equal parts and then laminate
- Gift Wrap: for a small gift or you can combine 2 pages
- Greeting cards or postcards: cut in half and fold for 2 cards
- Decoupage: shellac onto the surface of a box or other container

]Use your imagination to create unique fun items.
The sky and beyond is the limit!

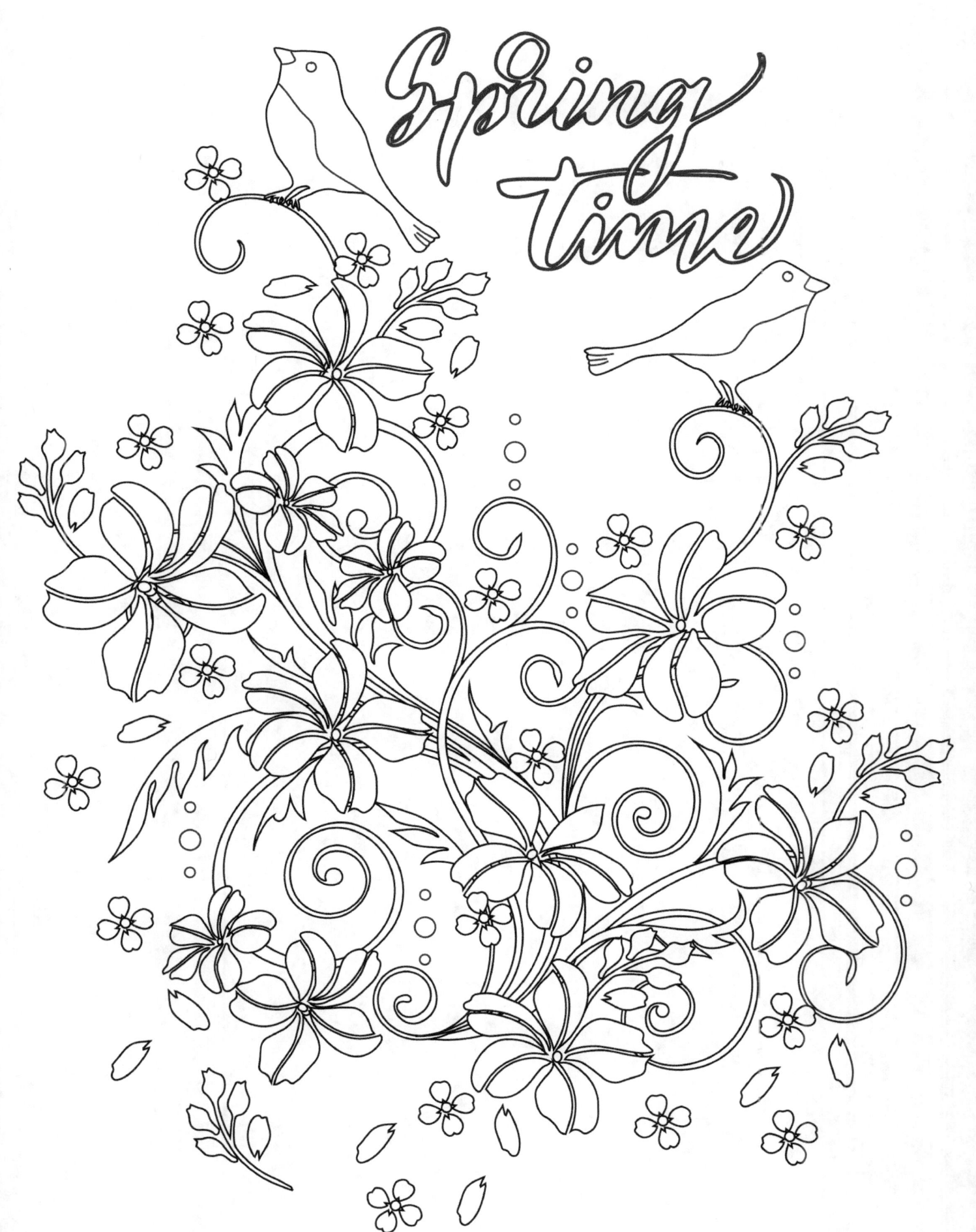

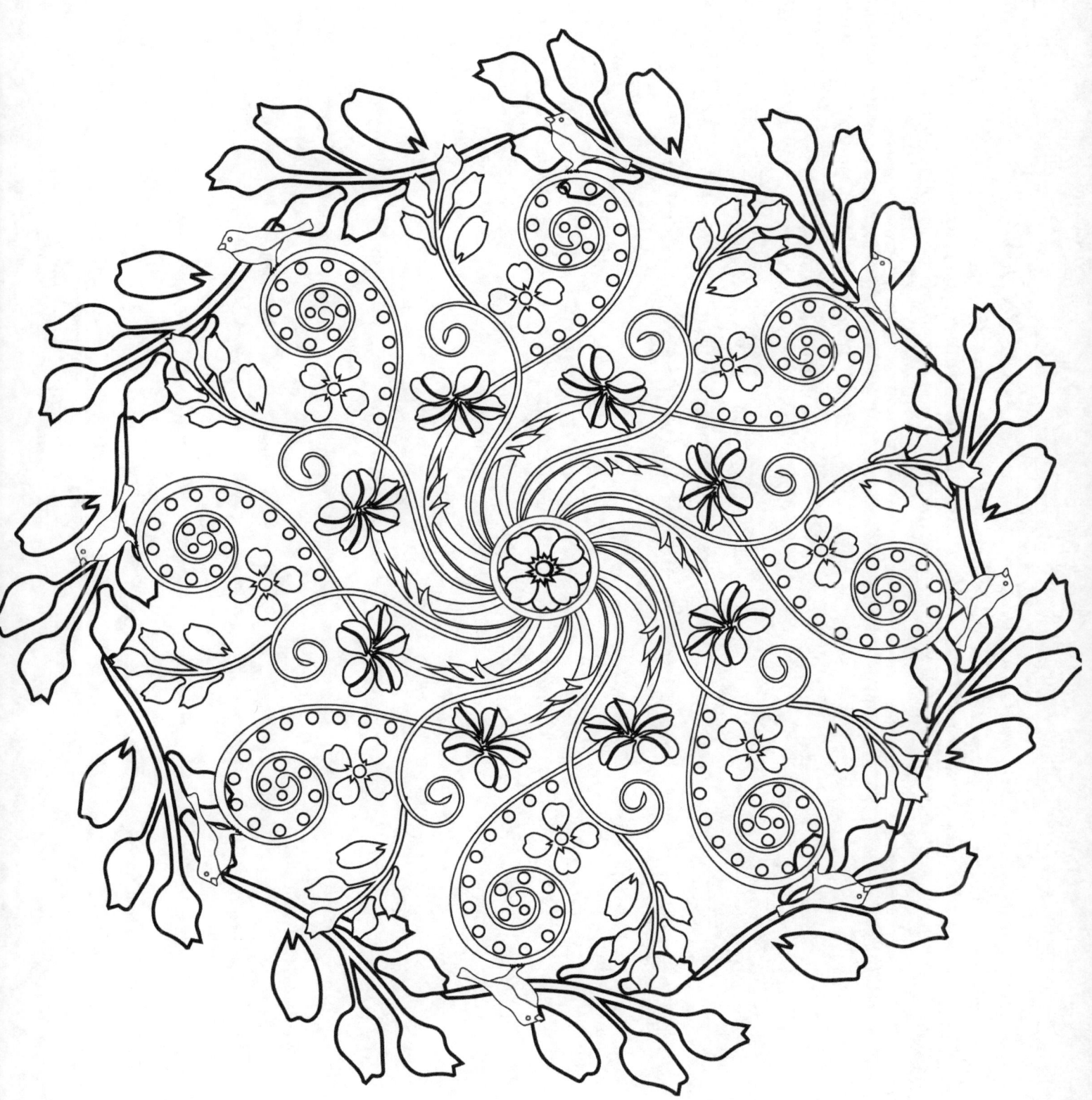

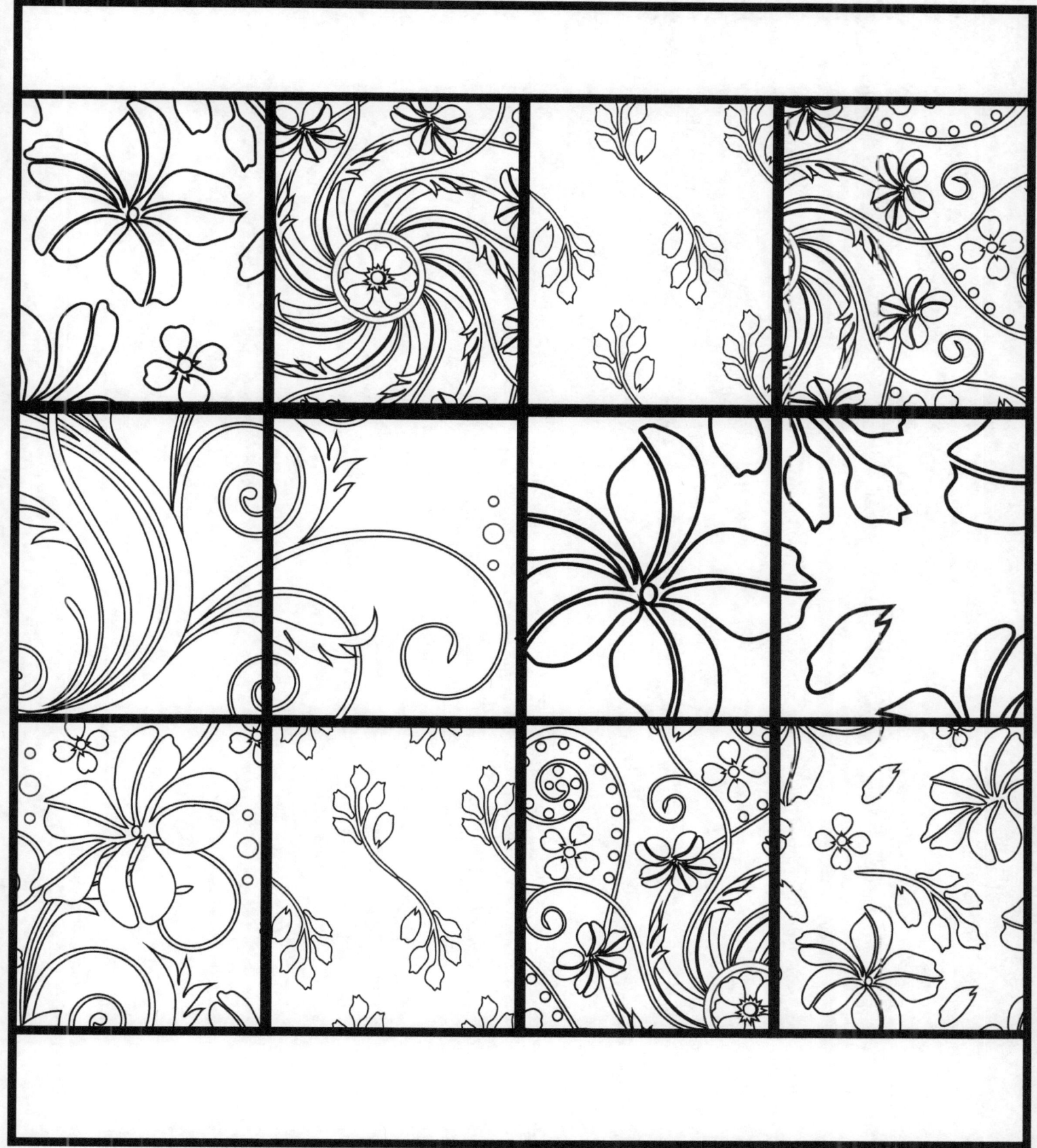

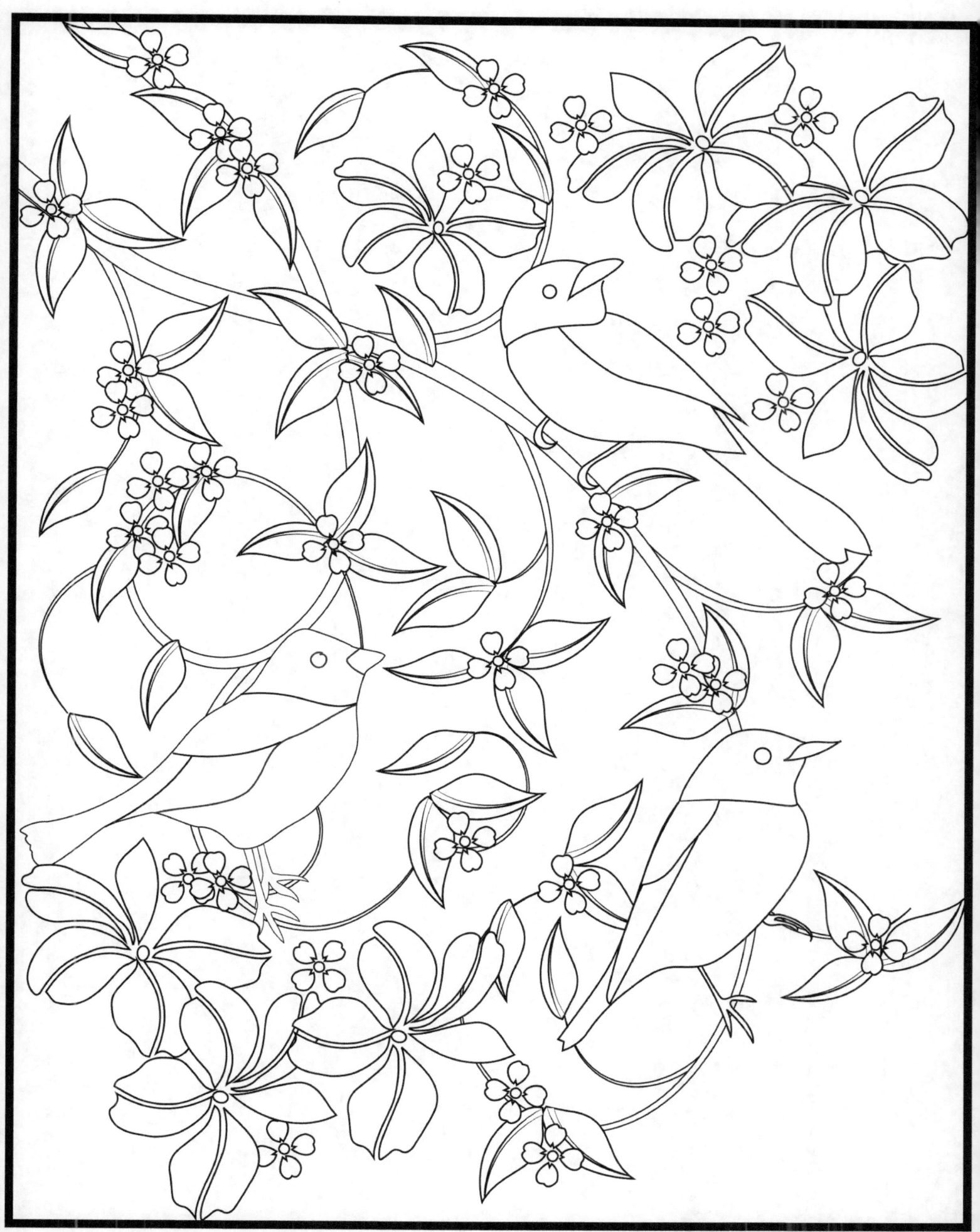

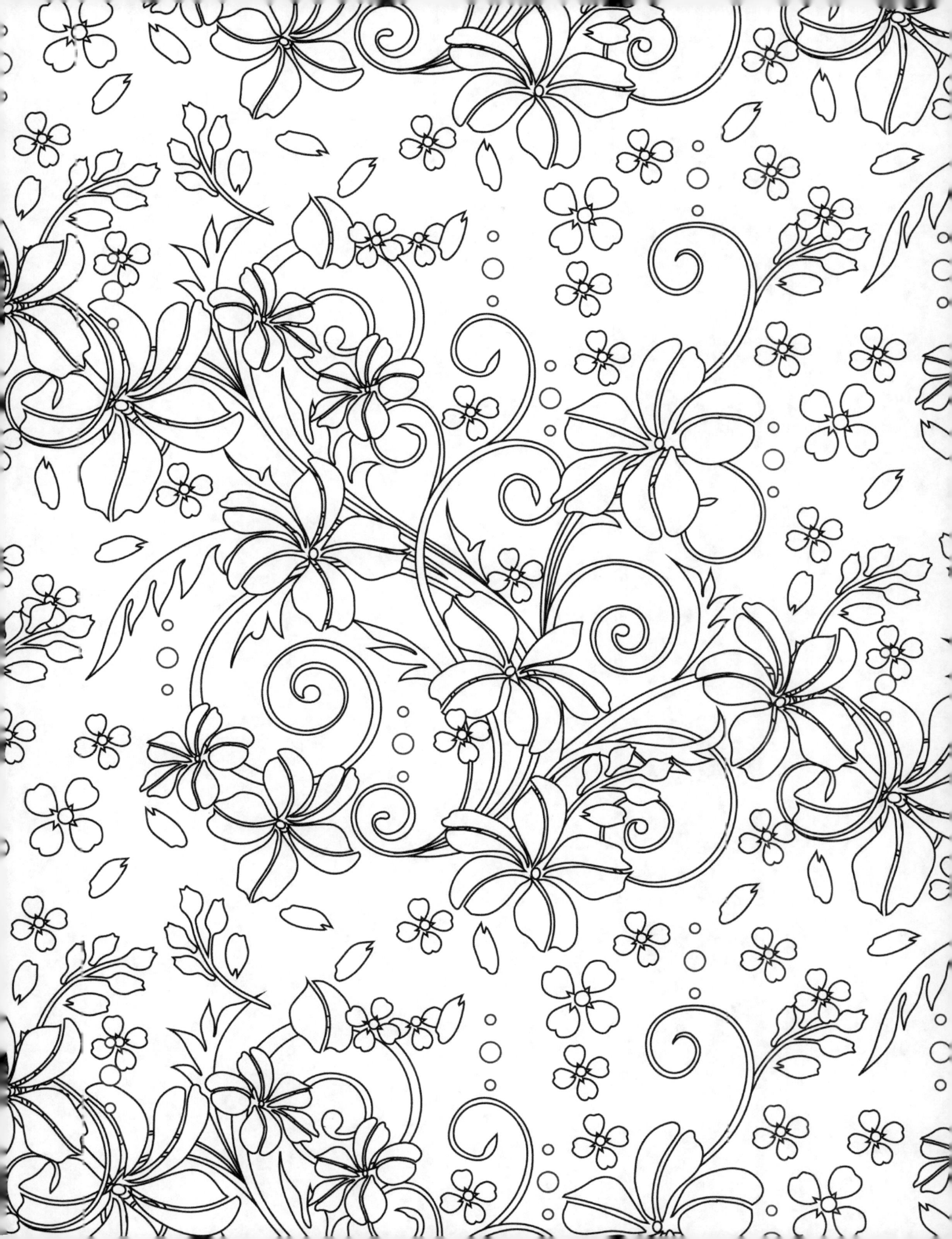

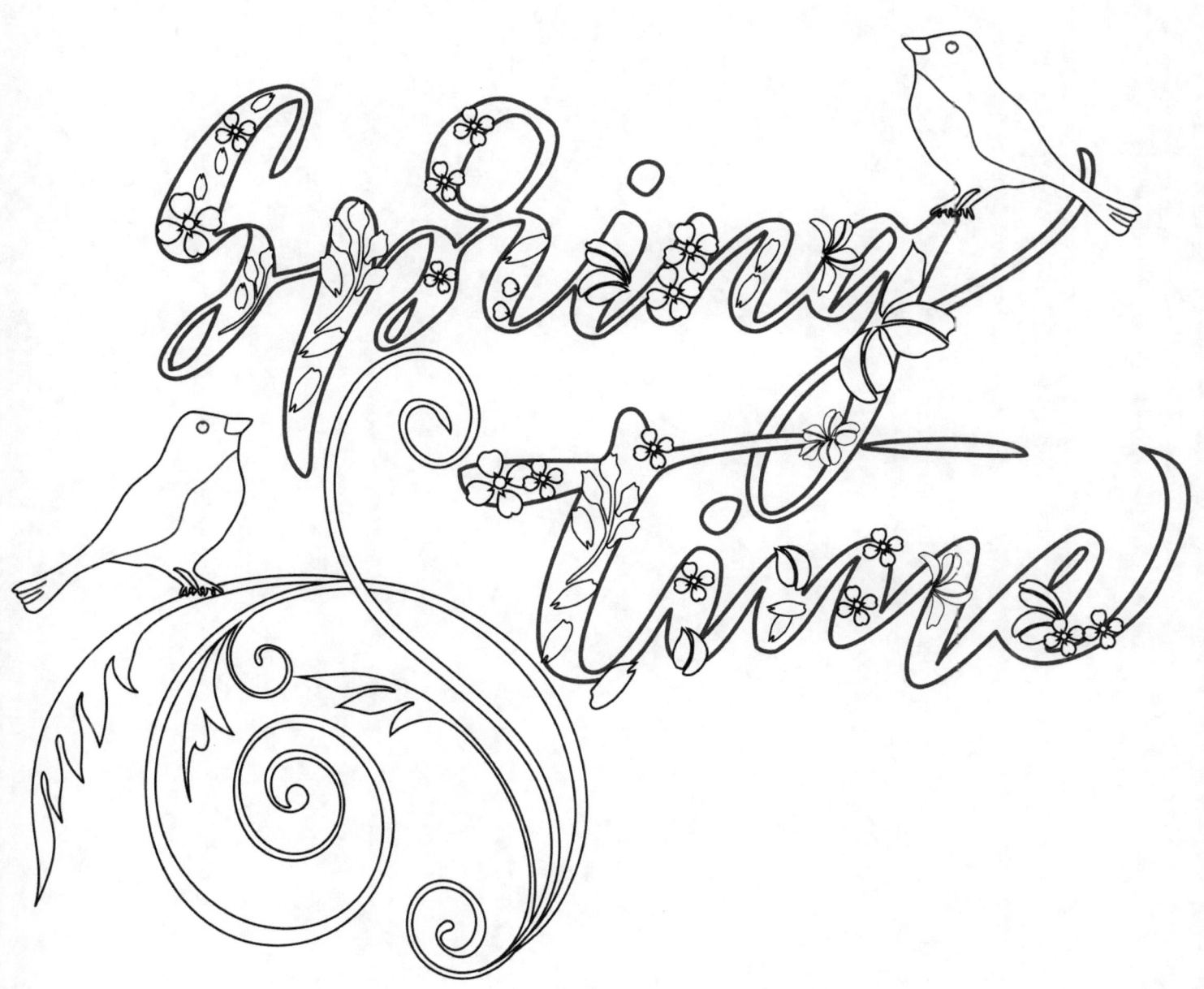

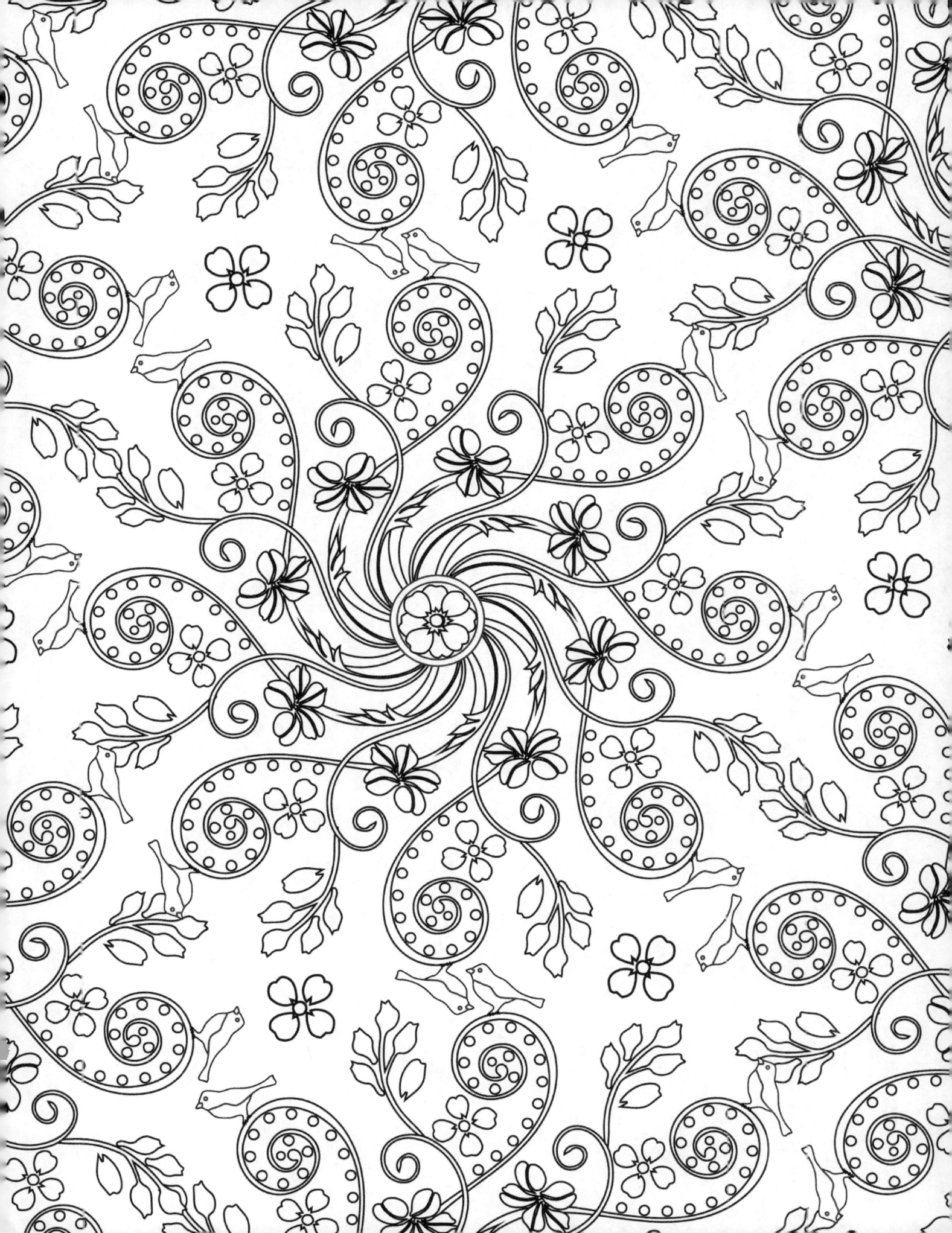

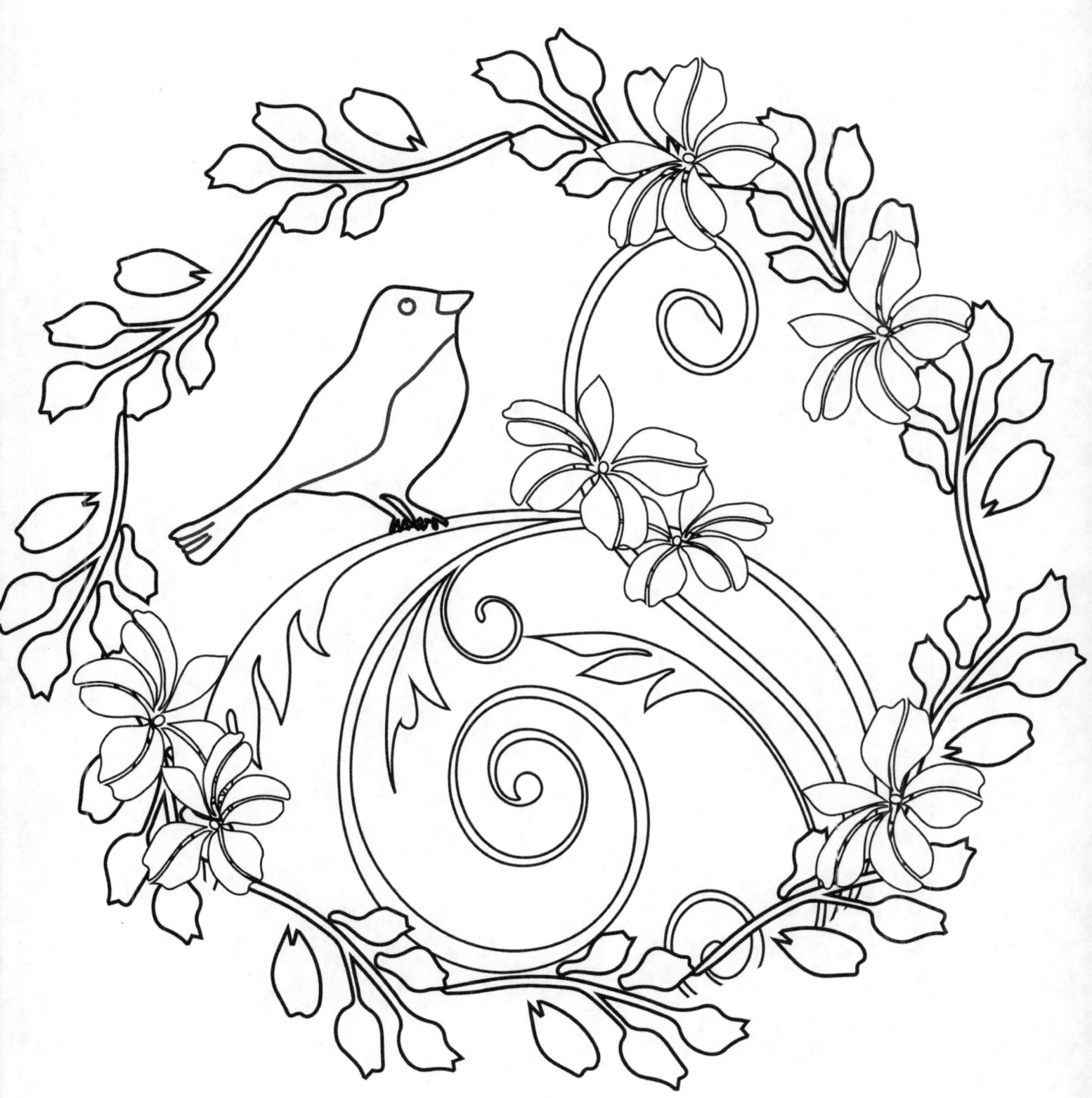

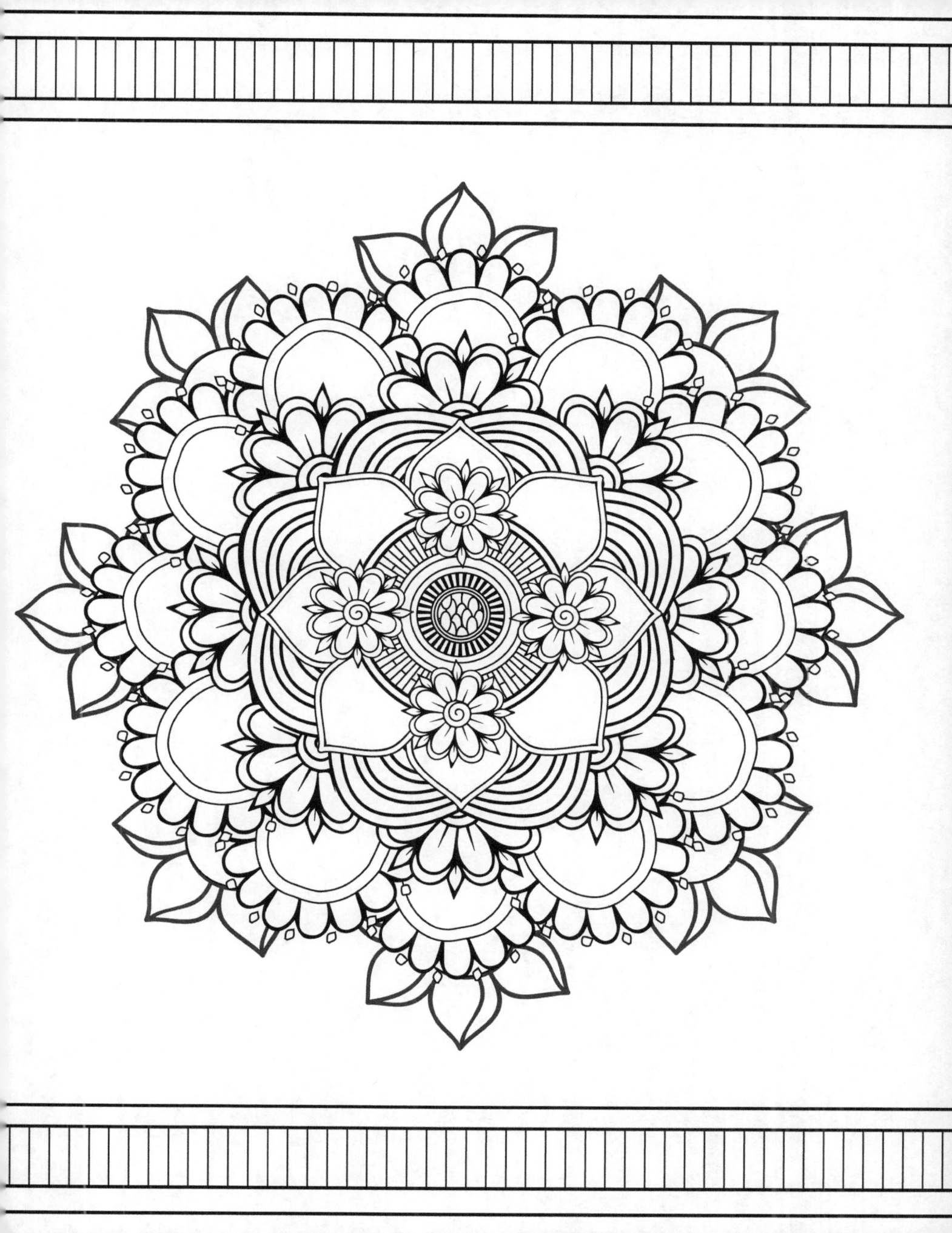

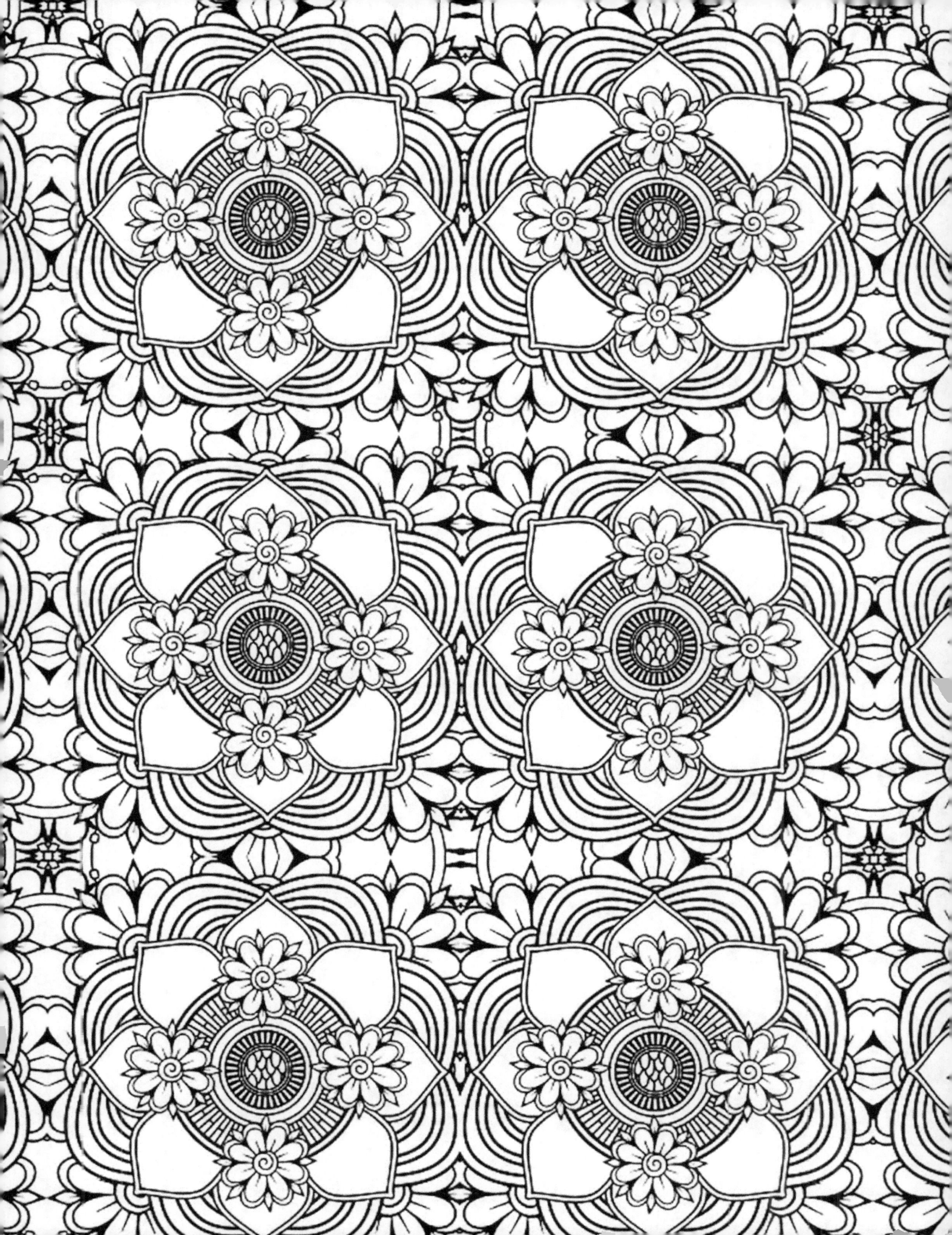

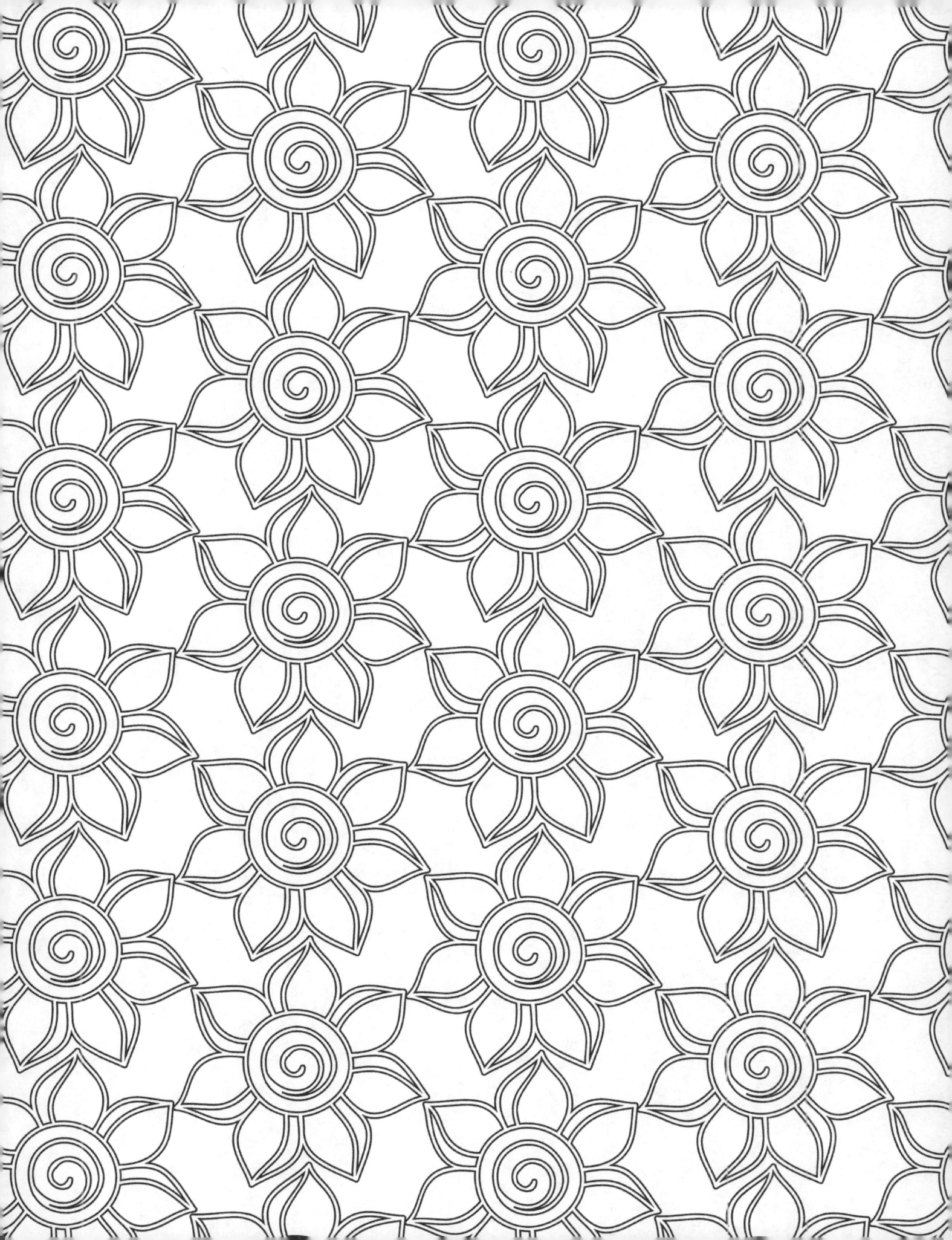

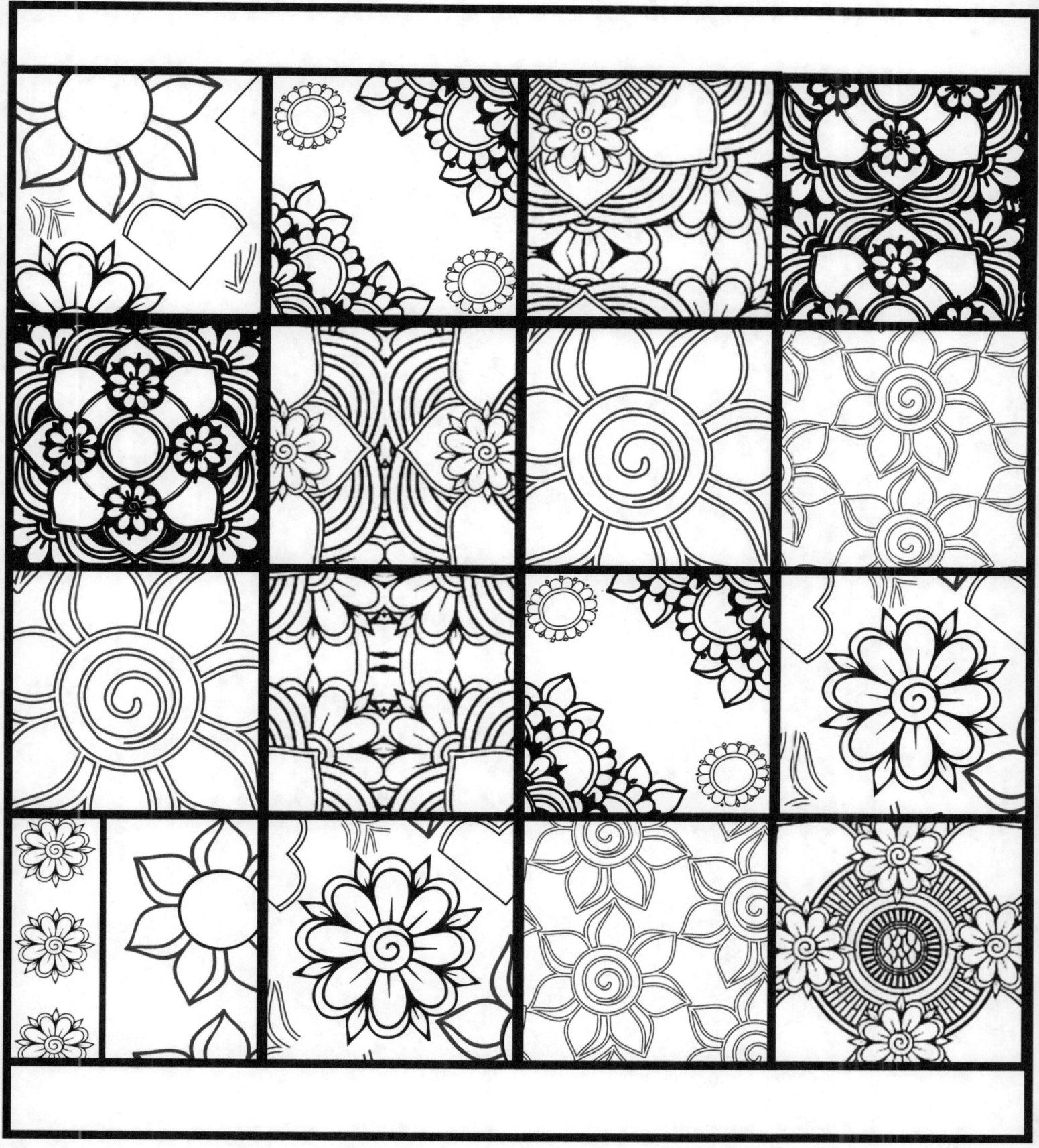

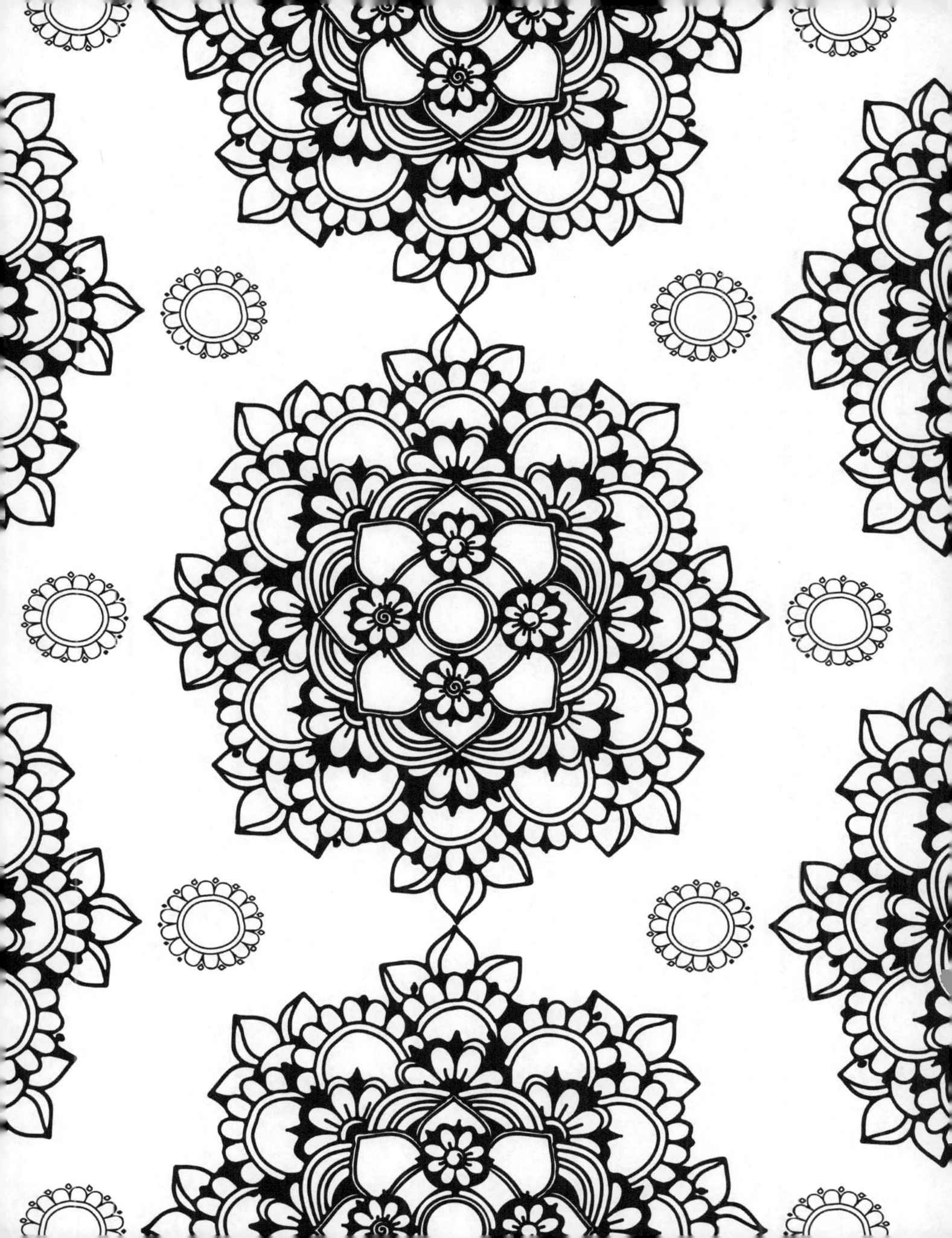

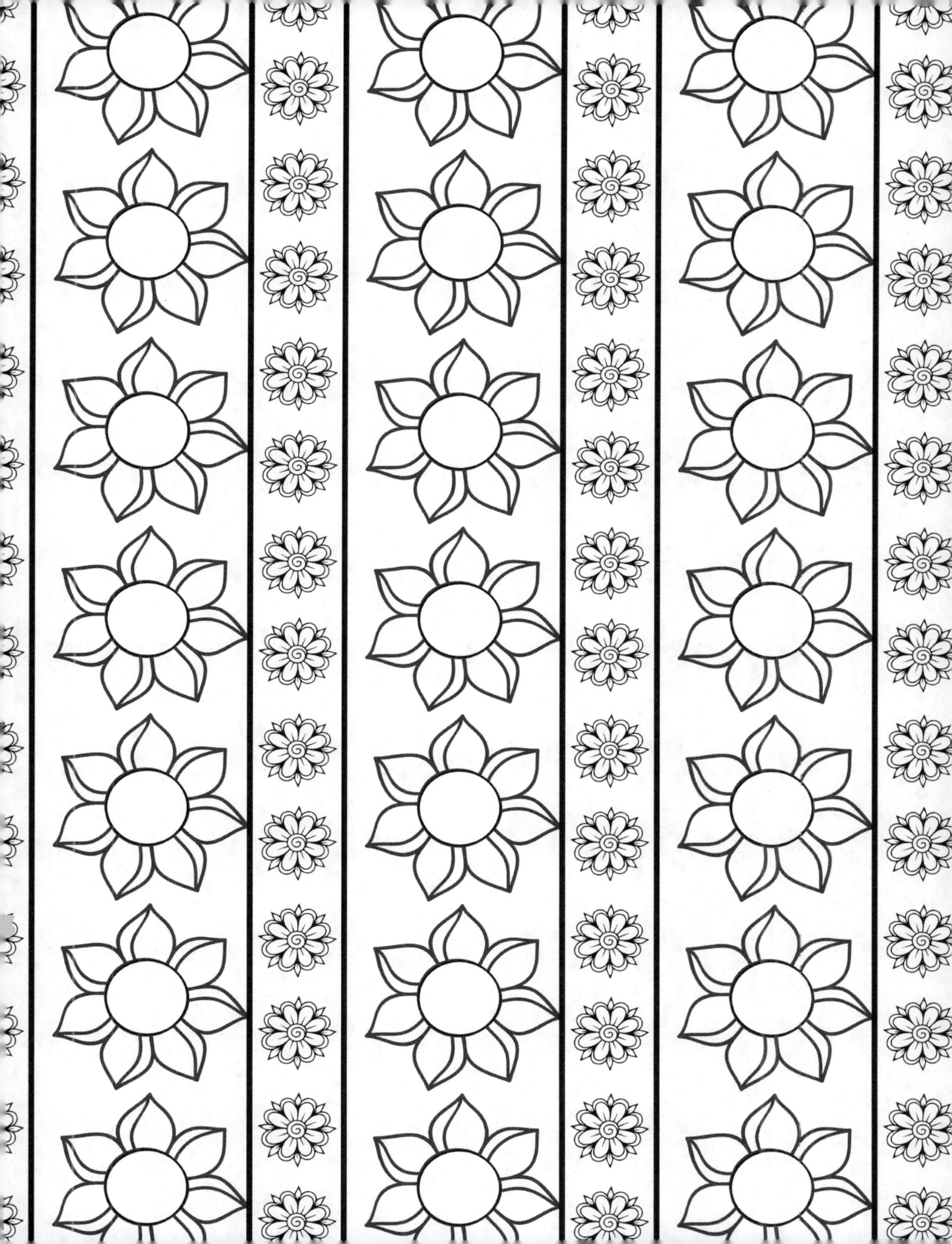